Cell Scientists

Discovering How Cells Work

Kimberly Fekany Lee, PhD

Life Science Readers: Cell Scientists: Discovering How Cells Work

Publishing Credits

Editorial Director
Dona Herweck Rice

Creative Director
Lee Aucoin

Associate Editor
Joshua BishopRoby

Illustration Manager
Timothy J. Bradley

Editor-in-Chief
Sharon Coan, M.S.Ed.

Publisher
Rachelle Cracchiolo, M.S.Ed.

Science Contributor
Sally Ride Science™

Science Consultants
Thomas R. Ciccone, B.S., M.A.Ed., Chino Hills High School
Dr. Ronald Edwards, DePaul University

Teacher Created Materials
5301 Oceanus Drive
Huntington Beach, CA 92649-1030
http://www.tcmpub.com

ISBN 978-0-7439-0584-8

Reprinted 2012
Printed in Malaysia
Thumbprints.42806

Table of Contents

Robert Hooke 4

Anton van Leeuwenhoek 8

Cell Theory 12

Hans Adolf Krebs 14

The Coris 16

Rita Levi-Montalcini 22

Cell Biologist: Elaine Fuchs 26

Appendices 28

- Lab: Make Your Own Light Microscope 28
- Glossary 30
- Index 31
- Sally Ride Science 32
- Image Credits 32

Robert Hooke (1635-1703)

Robert Hooke was born on the Isle of Wight in England. When he was a young boy, he had **smallpox.** He was scarred both physically and emotionally.

Something horrible happened when Hooke was 13 years old. His father, a clergyman, hanged himself. This added to the pain Hooke felt. He received an **inheritance** from his father. Then, he was sent off to London. He went to develop his artistic skills.

Isle of Wight

The Isle of Wight is in the British Isles. It is a beautiful island. It is diamond shaped and covered with trails and woodlands. You can take a ferryboat to get there.

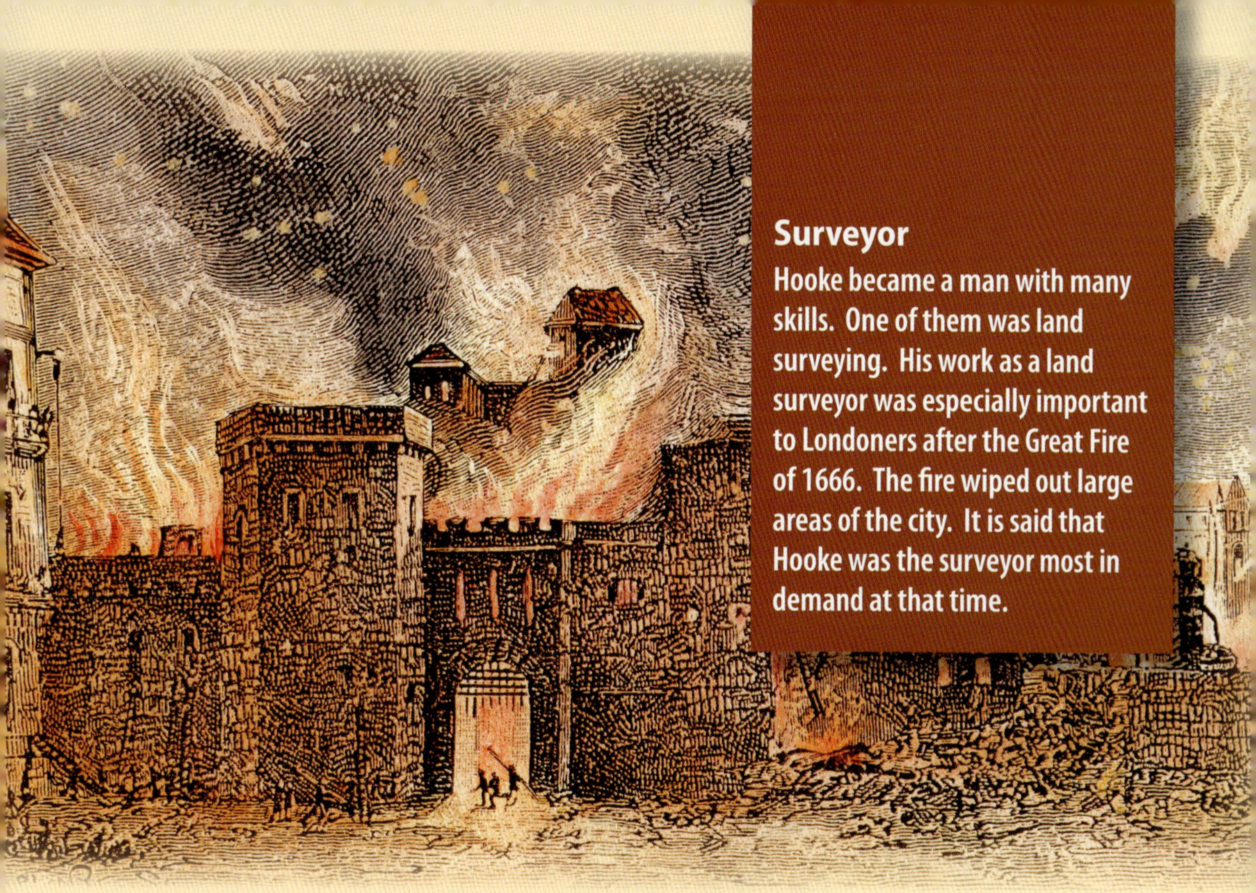

Surveyor

Hooke became a man with many skills. One of them was land surveying. His work as a land surveyor was especially important to Londoners after the Great Fire of 1666. The fire wiped out large areas of the city. It is said that Hooke was the surveyor most in demand at that time.

The Great Fire of London in 1666 raged for nearly one full week. It destroyed about 80 percent of the city. Just a few people died, but thousands became homeless.

When he was a boy, Hooke loved mechanical things. He was very smart. This helped him when he went to school. One teacher at school took a real interest in Hooke. The teacher saw how smart the boy was. He took Hooke under his wing. Hooke even lived with that teacher for a while.

Hooke worked as a servant to pay for his schooling. He went to Oxford University. While there, he became an assistant to a **physicist**. Together, they made an air pump. Then Hooke got another job. He did three or four experiments each week. He had to report on them to the Royal Society, an important group of scientists. It was the perfect job for him. Hooke got to use **chemistry, anatomy,** and **biology**. He kept this job for 41 years!

Hooke's drawing of cork cells

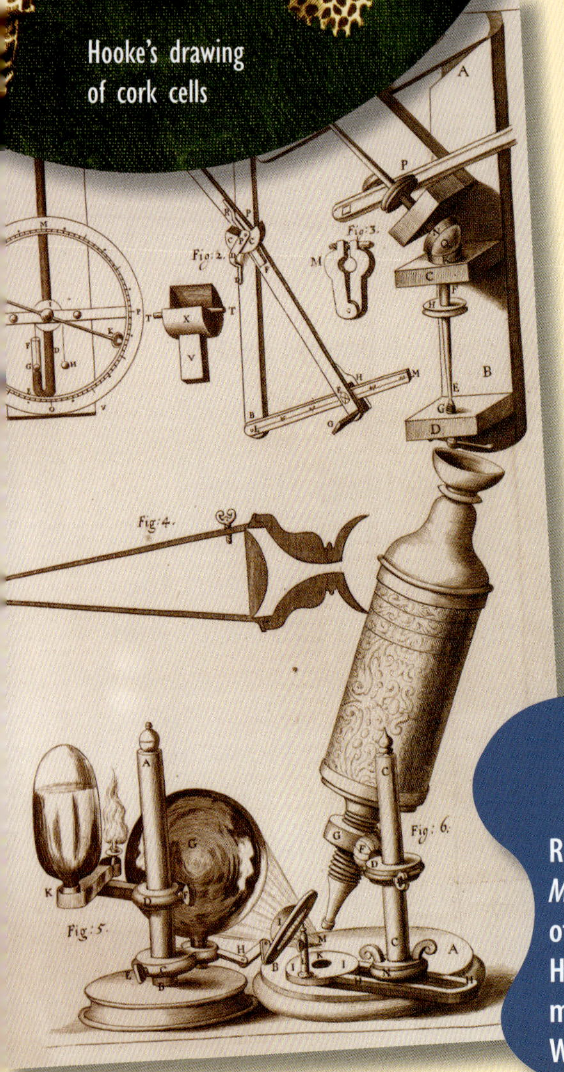

When he was 30 years old, Hooke invented a simple microscope. It is called the compound light microscope. It had three lenses. The microscope could magnify things 30 times their size. Hooke also built an early telescope.

Hooke examined many things. One of the things he looked at was a piece of cork. Cork is a kind of wood. It looks like rows of tiny boxes under the microscope. These tiny boxes reminded Hooke of something. He thought they looked like the tiny rooms, or cells, that **monks** lived in. So he named them **cells**. Hooke published his findings in his book *Micrographia*.

Hooke was the first scientist to observe cells and give them their name. But he did not understand how important cells were to the study of living things.

Have You Seen It?

Robert Hooke created a book called *Micrographia*. In it, he drew detailed images of his observations through a microscope. His handmade, leather, and gold-tooled microscope is on display at a museum in Washington, D.C.

Hooke was very smart. But he was also insecure. His physical looks probably had a lot to do with that. His scars and deformities grew worse with age. He was always in pain. Many people avoided him. Some made fun of him. That made Hooke's life sad and lonely. He never married. He died alone, blind and bedridden, when he was 67 years old.

Joan Wright Goodman (1925–2006)

Goodman studied stem cells and paved the way for modern research on them. A stem cell is a master cell in the human body, with the ability to grow into any cell type. Goodman also studied bone marrow transplants, their effects at fighting **radiation** damage, and the immune response in cells.

Goodman retired when she was 61, but she was far from done. She was full of energy and enthusiasm. She entered law school, got her law degree, and passed the bar exam. She decided not to practice law, though. Instead, she and her husband became supporters of the arts.

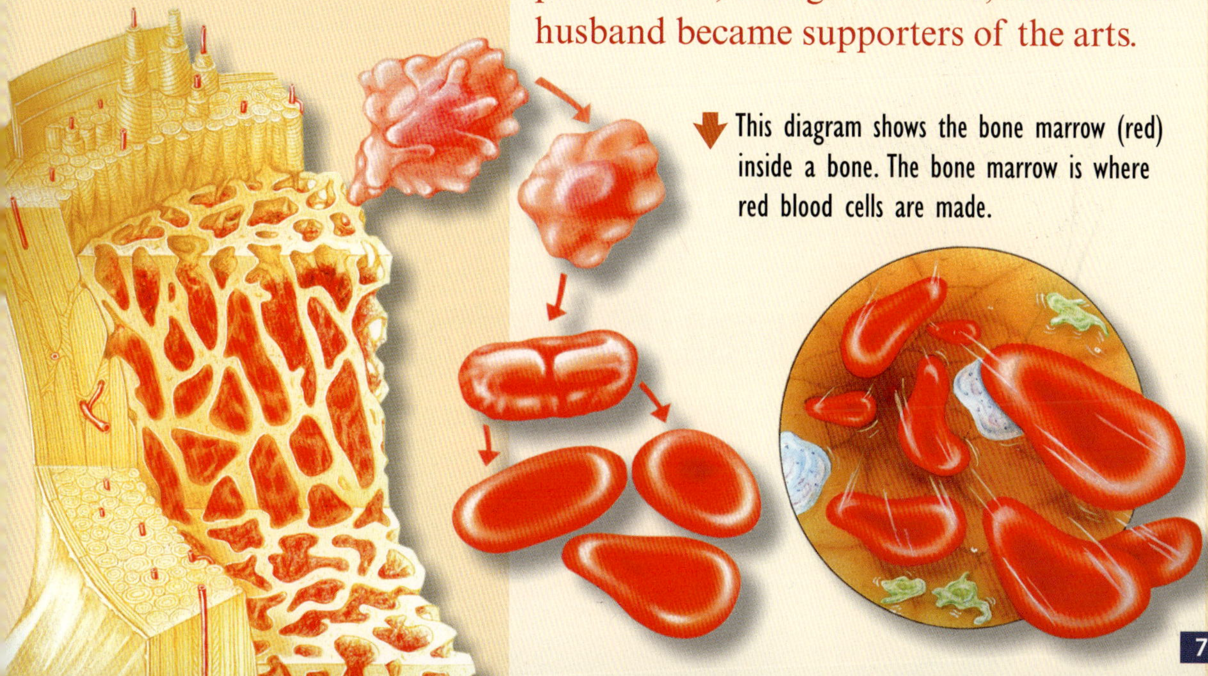

This diagram shows the bone marrow (red) inside a bone. The bone marrow is where red blood cells are made.

Anton van Leeuwenhoek (1632–1723)

Anton van Leeuwenhoek (AN-tahn vahn LEY-vuhn-hook) was born in Holland. His father was a basket maker. Leeuwenhoek only spoke Dutch. He never learned other languages.

He did not go to college at first. When he was 16, he became an apprentice. He worked with a linen draper and learned how to buy and sell fabric. By the age of 22, he returned to his hometown. He started his own business. He sold fabric. But he also had other jobs. Some jobs turned into whole businesses of their own. Eventually, he went to college.

It wasn't easy for Leeuwenhoek to become a scientist. He wasn't born with money. He wasn't given an education. He didn't speak other languages. But he was very curious, and he worked hard. When he was 48, other scientists finally recognized him as an equal. He joined the special group of scientists called the Royal Society for the Improvement of Natural Knowledge.

a representation of DNA strands

Christiane Nusslein-Volhard (1942–)

Christiane Nusslein-Volhard was born in Germany. She was very interested in plants and animals. She studied them with her family. After high school, she decided to study the sciences. She thought many of the classes were boring. But in her last year of school, she took a class on **genetics**. She thought that was interesting!

After graduation, Nusslein-Volhard worked in a laboratory. She studied DNA, among other things. DNA carries genetic information for living things. Nusslein-Volhard decided to study fruit flies. She learned that thousands of genes work together to control the development of fruit flies. She also looked at damaged genes. They caused birth defects in baby fruit flies.

Nusslein-Volhard's work is important. It can be applied to many things. It can even apply to humans. She won the Nobel Prize for her research on genes that cause birth defects.

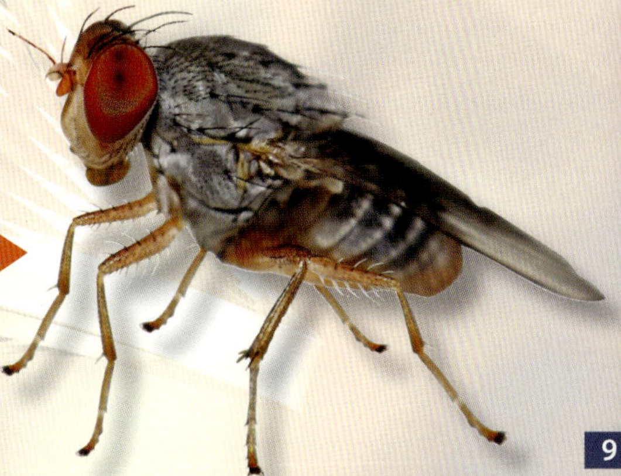

Christiane Nusslein-Volhard did research on fruit flies.

Leeuwenhoek hired an artist to draw his findings.

Leeuwenhoek's microscope

The blue specks are bacteria on the surface of a tooth.

Leeuwenhoek learned a valuable skill. He learned to make things out of glass. This came in handy. He made simple microscopes. He got interested in microscopes after seeing Robert Hooke's book. Hooke had included pictures. They fascinated Leeuwenhoek. He started to observe things with his microscopes.

Leeuwenhoek created one of the best microscopes of the time. He used it to study living organisms. He paid great attention to the things he saw. He wasn't a good artist. So, he hired someone to draw pictures of what he saw. He described things to the artist. He saw tiny veins with blood flowing through them. He also saw one-celled organisms in pond water.

Smile Now!

Leeuwenhoek made many interesting findings. One was on teeth. He looked at the plaque on his own teeth. He said it was as thick as batter. He also looked at the plaque on two ladies. And he looked at the teeth of two old men. The men had never cleaned their teeth! He found lots of little things moving around. In the old men, he found more than he could imagine. Do you know what he was seeing? He was among the first to see and tell about living **bacteria.**

Many Microscopes

Leeuwenhoek made more than 400 microscopes. Some of his microscopes could magnify things 200 times! Other microscopes of his day did much less. They could only magnify things about 20 to 30 times.

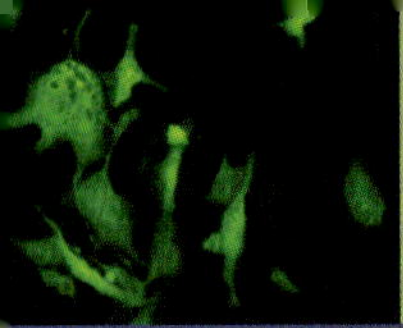

Cell Theory

1. All living things are made from one or more cells.

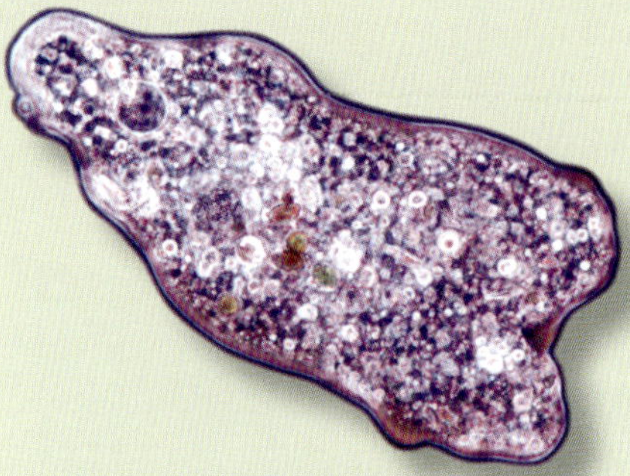

single-celled organisms

animal cell

plant cell

Fast forward almost 200 years. Three scientists were working on cells at about the same time. Their names were Matthais Schleiden (mah-TEE-ahs SHLAHYD-n), Theodor Schwann (TEY-oh-dawr shvahn), and Rudolf Virchow (ROO-dawlf FIR-koh). Together, their work became known as **Cell Theory**.

Schleiden worked with plant cells. Schwann worked with animal cells. One night, they had dinner together. They talked about their work. They realized that the cells they both studied were very similar. Plants and animals were both made of cells.

2. The cell is the basic unit of life.

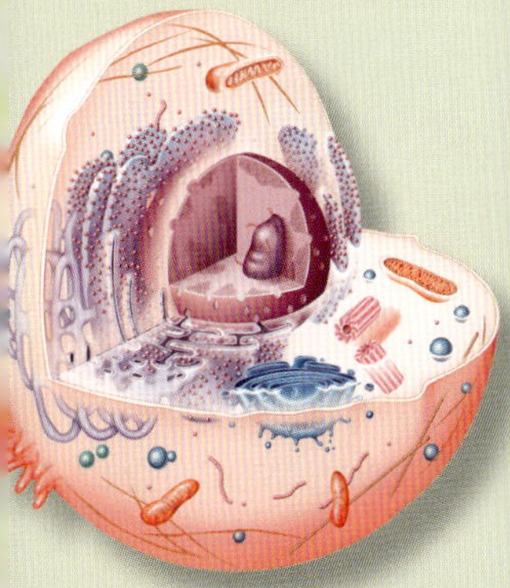

cell cross-section

3. All cells come from preexisting cells.

cell replication

They went to the laboratory and looked at cells. Then they published their findings in 1839. They said two important things. First, all living things are made of cells. Second, cells are the smallest part of a living thing that is itself alive.

The one thing that they weren't sure of was where cells came from. Almost 20 years later, Rudolf Virchow solved the puzzle. Cells, he said, come from other cells. This became the third part of Cell Theory.

Matthias Jakob Schleiden (1804–1881)

Matthias Jakob Schleiden was born in Germany. He was a botanist. However, botany was not his first career. He earned a law degree first. Then, he practiced law. Studying plants was at first only a hobby for Schleiden. He chose to use a microscope to study plant parts. He discovered that plants are made of cells. This discovery was the beginning of what is now known as **Cell Theory.** The cell theory consists of three main parts. His discovery was the beginning of the first part. That is, all plants are made of cells.

Hans Adolf Krebs (1900–1981)

Hans Adolf Krebs was born in Germany. He was the son of a Jewish doctor. He went to school to become a scientist. He specialized in biochemsitry. That is the study of how molecules interact inside living things.

In 1933, Hitler and the Nazi party took over Germany. They made it illegal for Jews to work as doctors. Krebs left the country. He continued his work in Britain.

The work paid off. Krebs figured out how cells turn glucose, or sugar, into energy the cells can use. Krebs won the Nobel Prize with his research partner.

Cells need energy. They use energy to work, to repair themselves, and to create new cells. They get that energy from a molecule called glucose.

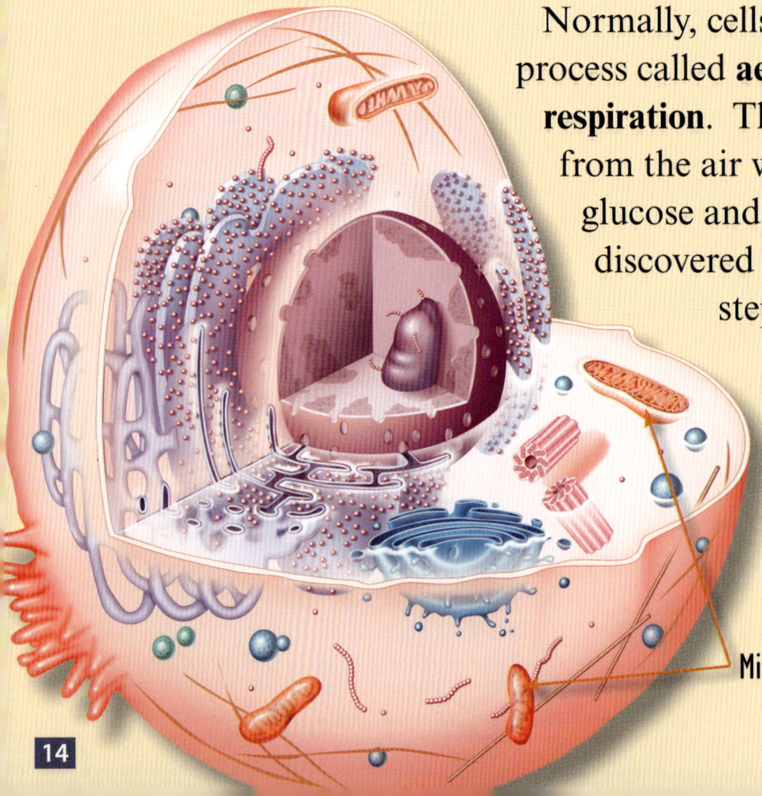

Normally, cells use glucose in a long process called **aerobic** (ai-ROH-bik) **respiration**. This process requires oxygen from the air we breathe. The cell takes glucose and slowly pulls it apart. Krebs discovered how the cell performs each step of taking apart glucose. He called it the Krebs Cycle.

Each time the cell pulls a chunk off of the glucose molecule, energy is

Mitochondria are where aerobic respiration occu

released. That energy is stored in a molecule called ATP. The aerobic respiration process produces 38 ATP from one glucose molecule!

Aerobic respiration is slow. It also requires lots of oxygen. Sometimes your body needs energy fast. Sometimes it doesn't have enough oxygen. Then it needs to do something different. It can't use the Krebs Cycle.

Knighthood

Krebs was knighted in the United Kingdom. **Knighthood** is awarded for public service and contributions to the nation.

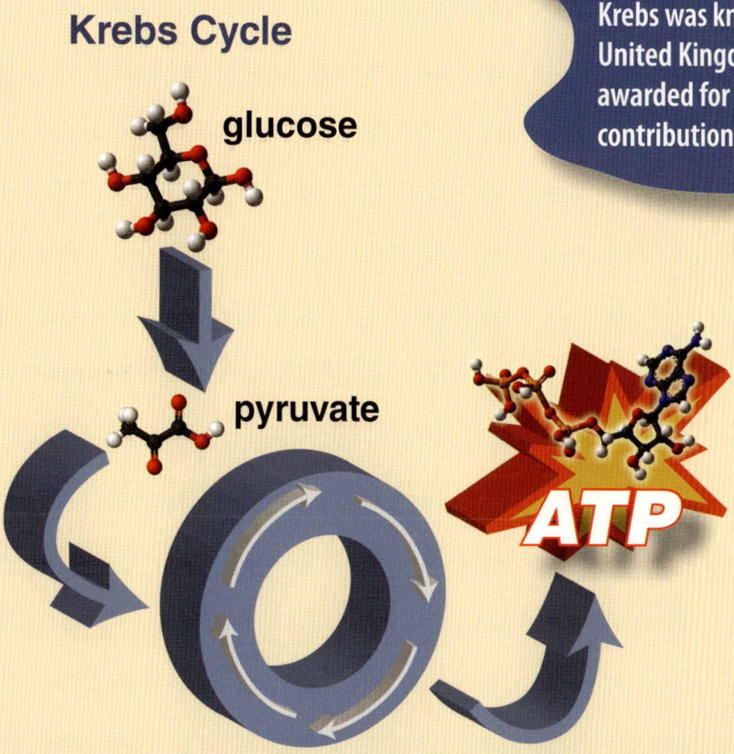

The Coris

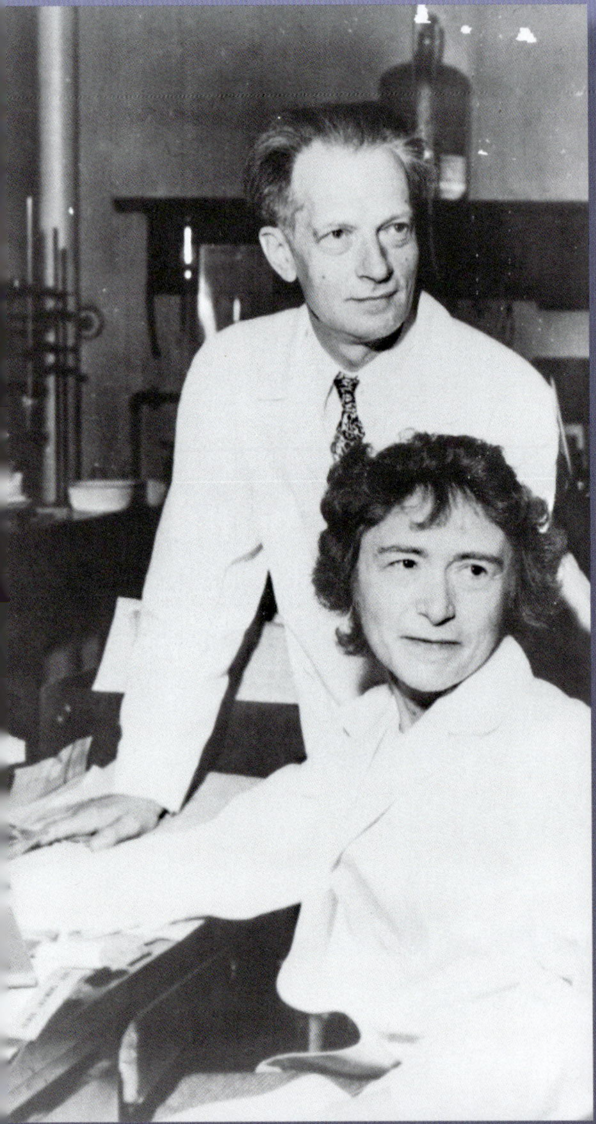

Gerty and Carl Cori

Gerty Theresa Radnitz (1896–1957) was born in Prague (prawg). At 10 years of age, she entered school. The schools for boys were different from those of girls. Boys were challenged with literature, science, and math. Girls were taught manners and handicrafts so they could be young ladies.

Radnitz (later Cori) became interested in science and math. She wanted to go to a university. To do so, she had to study science, math, and Latin. So, she went to a college-prep school. She did the whole program in two years.

Carl Ferdinand Cori (1896–1984) was born in Prague, too. His father and grandfather were scientists. This fostered his love of sciences. He began medical school when he was 18 years old.

That was where he met Gerty Radnitz. They both liked hiking and mountain climbing. They liked to garden, too. And they both wanted to be medical researchers. The two married.

To the Moon!

The Cori Crater on the far side of the moon is named after Gerty Cori.

World War I had just ended. Times were tough in Europe. Healthy food was scarce. Gerty Cori got sick. Her body was low on **nutrients** and vitamins. Times were especially hard for Jewish people. There was a lot of **prejudice**. So she and her husband decided to move to America.

Carl Cori left before his wife. He took a research job in New York. Six months later, Gerty Cori joined him. She was hired at the same lab. After six years in America, the Coris became U.S. citizens.

After nine years in New York, the Coris moved to Missouri. Carl Cori was hired as a professor at a medical school. Gerty Cori had the same degree and the same years of experience as her husband. Despite that, she was made a research assistant. It took 12 years for her to be made a professor!

Prague

Prague is in the Czech Republic. Its nickname is Heart of Europe.

Winners!

As of 2005, 758 individuals and 18 organizations had won the Nobel Prize. Of the 758 individuals, only 33 were women.

Nobel Couples

Besides the Coris, three other married couples share a Nobel Prize.

The Coris did most of their research together. When they wrote books, whichever of them did the most work would be listed first. In 1947, the Coris received a Nobel Prize. It was for their work on the Cori Cycle. The Cori Cycle is the cycling of molecules in the liver, blood, and muscle cells.

You already know about the Krebs Cycle, which makes 38 ATP but takes a long time. Sometimes, cells need energy fast. The slow process can't release energy quickly. The cells use a different process. It is called **anaerobic** (an-ai-ROH-bik) **respiration**.

liver cells

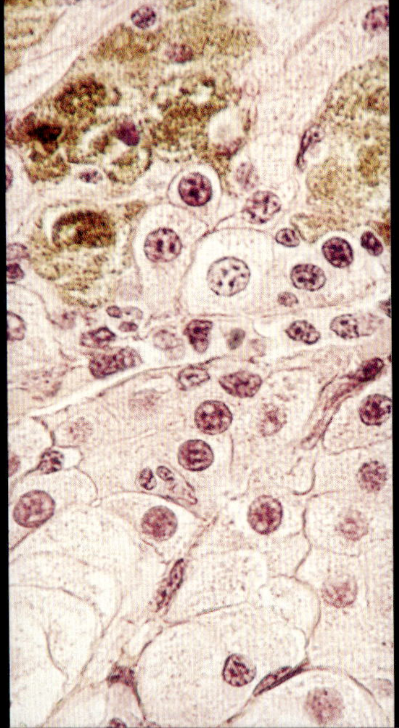

blood cells

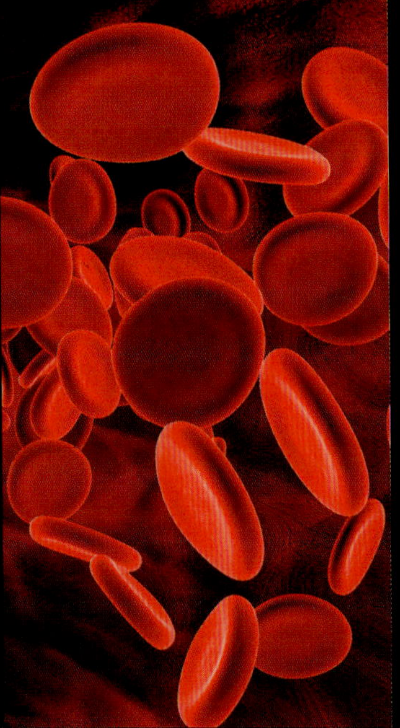

muscle cells

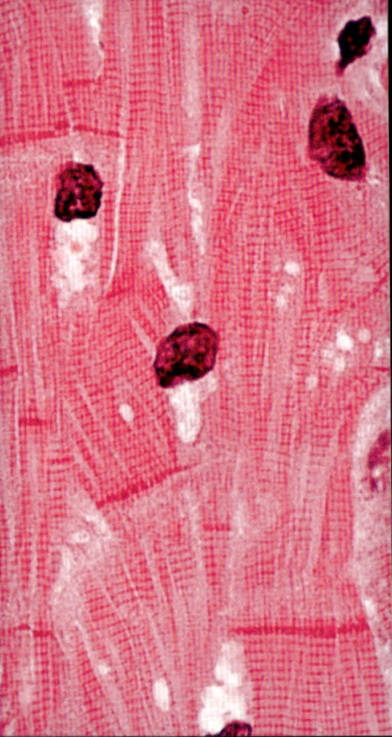

Anaerobic respiration is fast. It doesn't need oxygen. But it only makes two ATP. It is also messy. It produces a byproduct called lactate.

Lactate is a molecule. It still has energy inside it, but the cell can't release it. So cells release lactate by dumping it into the bloodstream. The Coris wanted to know what happened to the lactate next.

They followed the lactate as the blood took it to the liver. They found that the liver turns the lactate back into glucose. It takes six ATP to turn lactate back into glucose.

The Cori Cycle

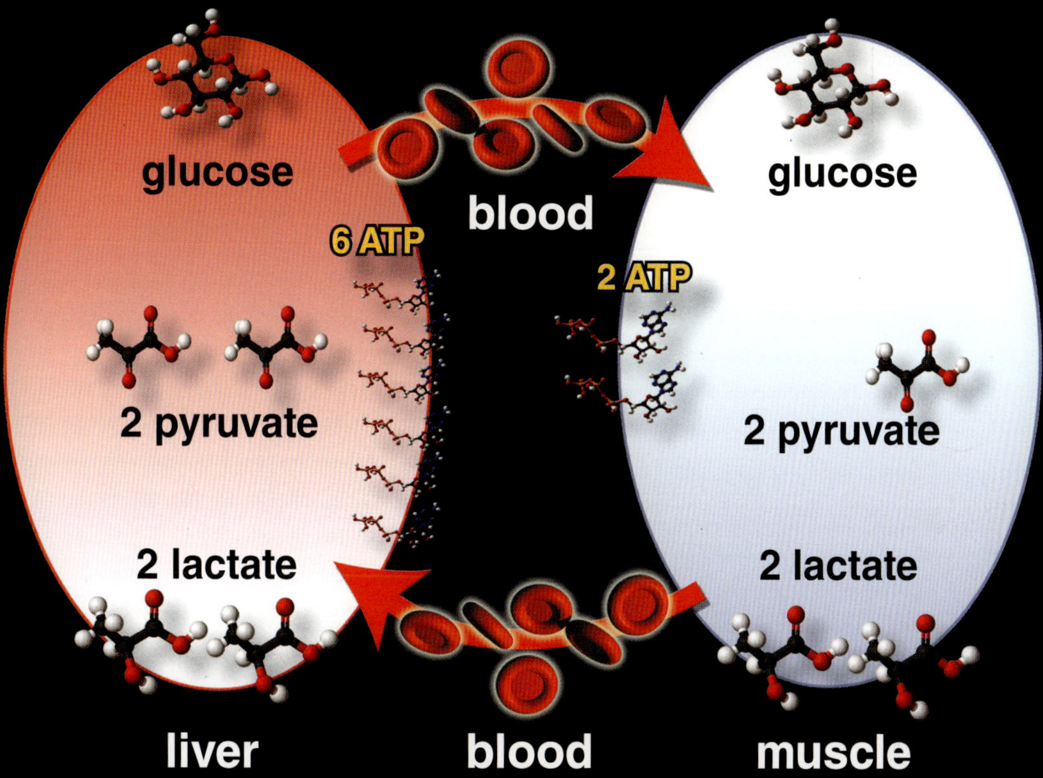

If you need a quick burst of energy, your cells use the quick and dirty method. This leaves lactate in your muscles and blood.

Cells have two ways of releasing energy from glucose. Aerobic respiration uses the Krebs Cycle to get the most out of glucose. Anaerobic respiration smashes apart glucose to get less energy faster. It leaves lactate behind. The Cori Cycle uses more energy to turn the lactate back into glucose.

You have probably felt the difference while playing sports or exercising. Most of the time, your cells are using aerobic respiration. They have the time to get all 38 ATP out of the glucose. If you start using more energy, though, your cells need more oxygen for the Krebs Cycle. You start breathing harder to get more air and more oxygen.

Then, your cells use up all the oxygen you bring in. If they still need more energy, they start using anaerobic respiration. It doesn't need oxygen. Anaerobic respiration only produces two ATP, but it does it fast. Your cells can do it over and over again very quickly. Your cells get the energy that they need.

All that quick energy comes at a price, though. Anaerobic respiration makes lactate. For every two ATP it makes, it makes two lactate molecules, too. The Cori Cycle takes the lactate to the liver. The liver uses six more ATP to make the two lactate molecules into a glucose molecule.

So, you get two ATP right away. Later, you have to use six more ATP. Over all, anaerobic respiration means you lose four ATP!

The important thing is that you got the ATP when you needed it. Imagine that you hurried to slide into home or you drove down the field for the goal. Later, after the run is made or the goal is scored, your body can use the Krebs Cycle and aerobic respiration to supply the ATP to turn lactate back into glucose. This is why you may feel tired or really hungry after lots of exercise. Your cells are still paying for all that anaerobic respiration!

Sore Muscles and Lactate

Have you ever exercised so hard that you were sore afterward? Some biologists think that lactate is to blame. If your cells are using anaerobic respiration, they create a lot of lactate. The lactate can build up in your muscle cells. There might be so much lactate that the cells bulge out and squeeze nerve cells. This might be why you ache after exercising.

Other biologists are not so sure. They don't think there is enough lactate to cause muscle cells to bulge. Muscle aches last longer than the lactate does, too. If the lactate gets carried away by the blood, the aching should stop.

If you become a biochemist like Krebs and the Coris, maybe you can find out what makes muscles ache!

Lactate may be to blame for sore muscles.

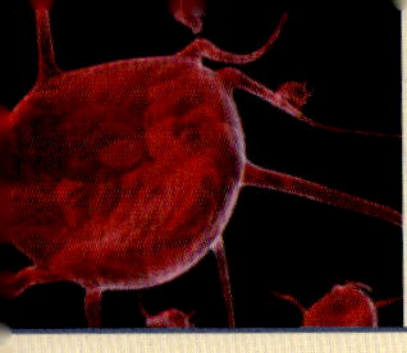

Rita Levi-Montalcini (1909–)

Rita Levi-Montalcini (LEE-vee-mon-tuhl-CHEE-nee) was born in Turin, Italy. She was one of four children. She had only one brother. She and her twin sister were the youngest.

Rita Levi-Montalcini

Levi-Montalcini's family life was filled with love. Both her parents were very smart. But her family was traditional. That meant that her father was the head of the household. He made the decisions. He loved his family, and he respected women. However, he thought that the most important jobs for women were to be wives and mothers. He believed that a career would get in the way of these roles. His own two sisters had advanced degrees. They found it hard to be wives and mothers and to have careers. For these reasons, he did not allow his daughters to further their educations.

Levi-Montalcini's intelligence made this a very difficult decision for her. She wanted to learn, and she had the ability to go far.

Turin is a beautiful city in northwest Italy. It is surrounded on two sides by the Alps. In 2006, it was home to the Olympic Games.

The lack of education was fine for Levi-Montalcini's twin sister. She was a gifted artist. She was able to pursue her goals. It was harder for Levi-Montalcini. Her father finally allowed her to go to school. She studied Latin, Greek, and math. She graduated from high school in eight short months! Then, she enrolled in medical school. She graduated from medical school at the top of her class.

After a few years, World War II was in full swing. Jews were no longer allowed to practice medicine in Italy. Levi-Montalcini built a small lab in her bedroom. She continued her research on chick **embryos**. When the war worsened, she moved her lab many times. She moved it into a basement. She even moved it out to the country.

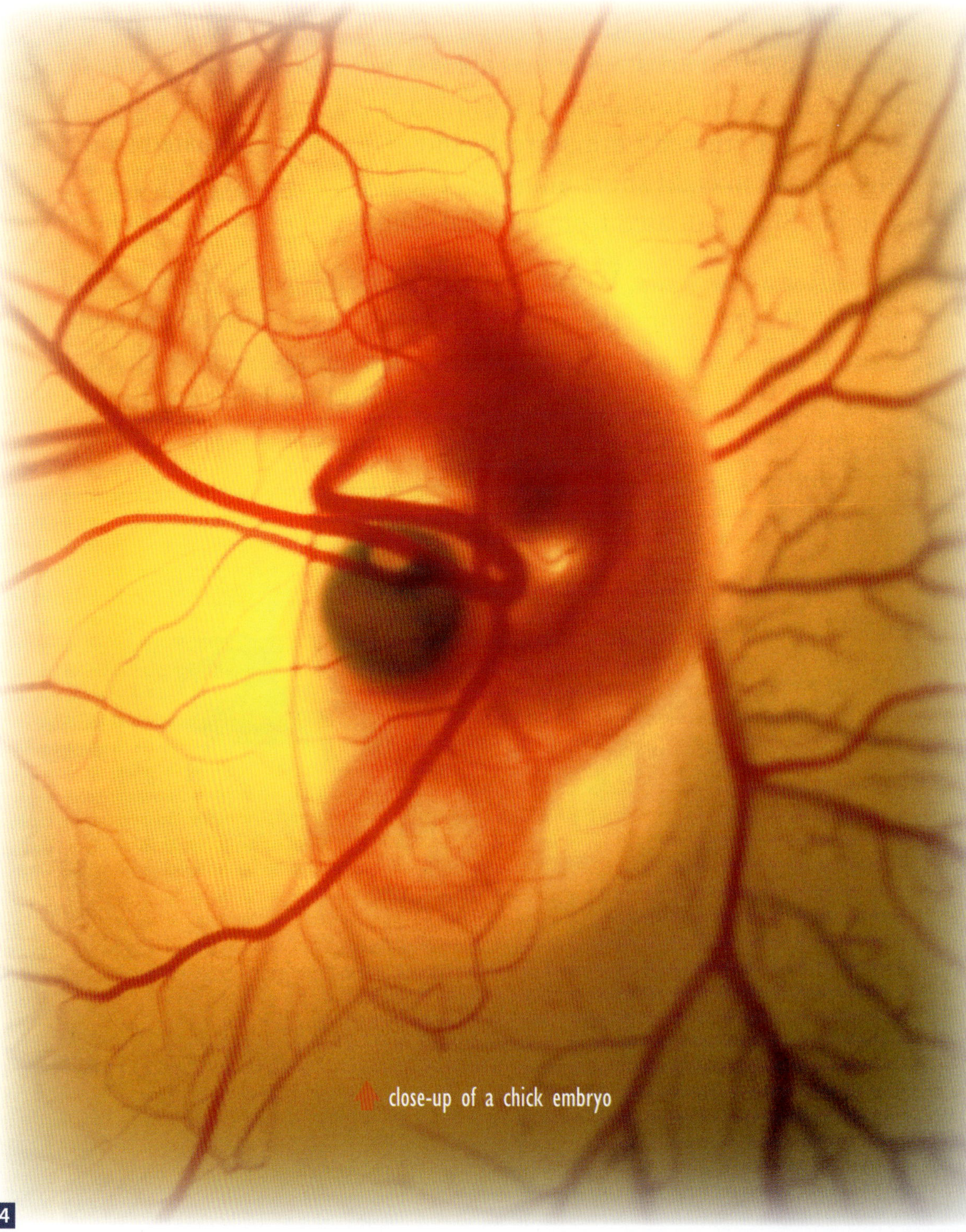

close-up of a chick embryo

Toward the end of the war, Levi-Montalcini was hired as a medical doctor. She worked with people who had become ill during the war. After the war, she became a professor in Turin. Then she got an offer from a researcher in the United States. She joined him in conducting more experiments with chick embryos. She planned to stay in the country for just a few months. But then she became a professor of **zoology** and biology. She split her time between the United States and Italy. She started a research unit in Rome.

Today, she lives in Italy. The president of Italy made her a Senator for Life! Now she splits her time between science and politics—and visiting her family.

Levi-Montalcini researched many things. She might be best known for her study of chemicals that help cells grow. She received many awards for her work, including a Nobel Prize.

Stanley Cohen (1922–)

Stanley Cohen was born in Brooklyn, New York. He received his Ph.D. in biochemistry. Cohen is most known for the research he conducted with Levi-Montalcini. They discovered and studied chemicals that stimulate cell growth. Those chemicals are often called **growth factors.** Cohen named their discovery **epidermal** growth factor, or EGF. Together, Cohen and Levi-Montalcini shared the Nobel Prize for their work on growth factors.

Cell Biologist: Elaine Fuchs

Rockefeller University

Skin Smarts

Can science be cute? It sure can. One of Elaine Fuchs' projects is a super-fuzzy mouse. It has much more hair than it should. Why? Fuchs studies special cells. And she's learned how to make the cells either become skin or grow hair. Her discoveries may someday help treat people with skin diseases, baldness, or cancer.

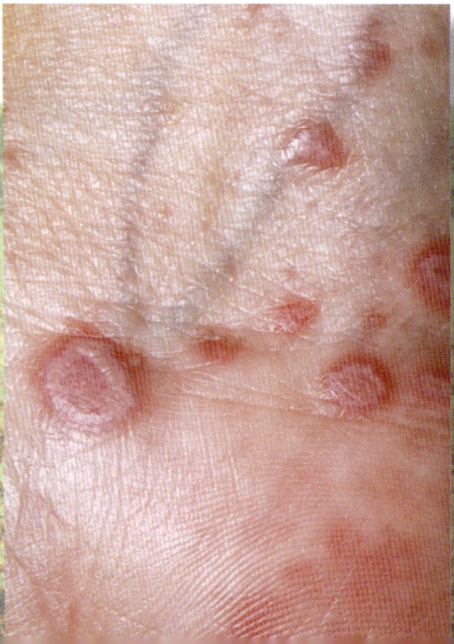

"The most rewarding part of my job as researcher is the adventure of discovering something that no one else has known before," Fuchs says.

Fuchs grew up with many scientists in her family, but she says she probably would have become a scientist anyway. "Most of my interest in science really came from playing in the fields and catching butterflies and climbing trees. Science is all around us." Catch it if you can!

4 U 2 Do

"All we have to do is look at our own body and realize that science is a part of us," Fuchs says. Can you find any science in your body?

Think About It

If you could treat any disease, what disease would you treat? What kinds of questions would you ask to get started?

Did U Know?

The special cells Fuchs studies are called stem cells. Some stem cells have the ability to become skin, muscle, or even brain cells.

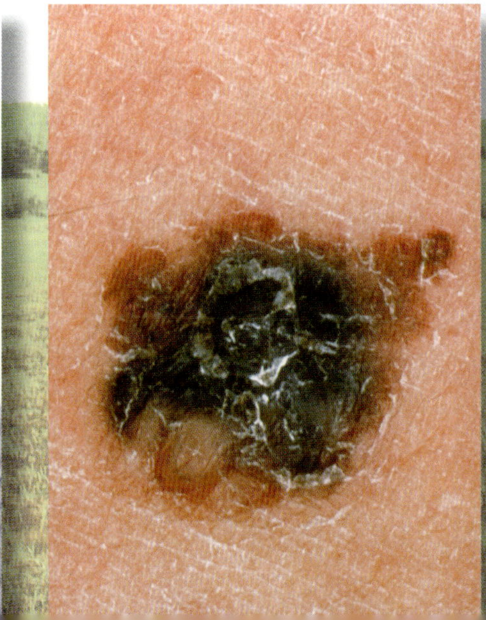

Fuchs's research is working to make a difference for those battling skin diseases (far left), baldness (middle), and skin cancer (near left).

Lab: Make Your Own Light Microscope

Make this simple light microscope to see how early biologists examined their specimens.

Materials

- two magnifying glasses
- a newspaper article
- a photograph
- a paper and pen to record your results

Procedure

1 Hold one magnifying glass just above the surface of the newspaper article. Then, hold it above the photo. The print and image should appear larger.

2 Move the magnifying glass higher. See how the print and photo change. They should become blurred as you move the magnifying glass higher.

3 Return the magnifying glass to the original position. Place it just above the newspaper article.

4 Get the second magnifying glass. Place it between the first magnifying glass and your eyes.

5 Move the second magnifying glass up and down. Get the print in clear focus. How does it look?

6 Describe what happens. Does it appear larger or smaller than it did when you used a single magnifying glass?

7 Record your results.

8 Repeat, using the photograph.

Glossary

aerobic respiration—slow process through which cells get energy

anaerobic respiration—process through which cells get energy quickly

anatomy—the scientific study of the body and how its parts are arranged

bacteria—plural for bacterium, a type of very small organism that lives in air, water, earth, plants, and animals, often one that causes a disease

biology—the science that studies living organisms

cell—the smallest unit of living things

cell theory—states that all living things are made of cells, all cells come from other cells, and cells are the basic unit of all living things

cellular respiration—process used by cells to break down food molecules into small units of energy

chemistry—the science that studies the makeup and properties of substances and the forms of matter

embryo—an animal that is developing either in its mother's womb or in an egg

epidermal—pertaining to the epidermis, the outermost layer of the skin

genetics—a branch of biology that involves studying heredity and genetic variations

growth factors—chemicals that stimulate cell growth

inheritance—money or objects

knighthood—the rank of a knight

monk—a member of a group of religious men who do not marry and usually live together in a monastery

nutrients—any substance that plants or animals need in order to live and grow

physicist—a person who studies physics (the scientific study of matter and energy and the effect that they have on each other)

prejudice—an irrational hatred, fear, or distrust of a person or group

radiation—the process of giving off energy

smallpox—an acute, highly infectious, often fatal disease caused by a poxvirus and characterized by high fever and aches with subsequent widespread eruption of pimples that blister, produce pus, and form pockmarks

zoology—the scientific study of animals

Index

anatomy, 5
ATP molecule, 15, 18–21
bacteria, 11
biology, 5, 25
botany, 13
cells, 6–7, 12–15, 18–21, 25–27
cell theory, 12–13
cellular respiration, 14
chemistry, 5
Cohen, Stanley, 25
compound light microscope, 6, 28–29
Cori, Carl Ferdinand, 16–21
Cori Crater, 17
Cori Cycle, 18–21
Cori, Gerty Theresa, 16–21
DNA, 8–9
embryos, 23–24
epidermal, 25
epidermal growth factor (EGF), 25
Fuchs, Elaine, 26–27
genes, 9
genetics, 9
Goodman, Joan Wright, 7
growth factors, 25
Hooke, Robert, 4–7
Krebs, Hans Adolf, 14–15 , 21
Krebs Cycle, 14–15, 18, 20–21
Levi-Montalcini, Rita, 22–25
microscope, 10–11, 13, 28–29
monks, 6
Nazi Germany, 14
Nobel Prize, 9, 14, 18, 25
Nusslein-Volhard, Christiane, 9
nutrients, 17
physicist, 5
prejudice, 17
radiation, 7
Schleiden, Matthias Jakob, 12–13
simple microscope, 10–11, 28–29
smallpox, 4
stem cell, 7, 27
van Leeuwenhoek, Anton, 8–11
zoology, 25

Sally Ride Science

Sally Ride Science™ is an innovative content company dedicated to fueling young people's interests in science. Our publications and programs provide opportunities for students and teachers to explore the captivating world of science—from astrobiology to zoology. We bring science to life and show young people that science is creative, collaborative, fascinating, and fun.

Image Credits

Cover: Bernard Becker Medical Library; p.3 Photos.com; p.4 (top) Digital Wisdom/Mountain High Maps; p.4 (left) The Granger Collection, New York; p.4 (bottom) mediacolor's/Alamy; p.5 The Granger Collection, New York; p.6 (top) Omikron/Photo Researchers, Inc.; p.6 Library of Congress; p.7 Michel Gilles/Photo Researchers, Inc.; p.8 (top) Kirsty Pargeter/Shutterstock; p.8 (left) Hulton Archive/Getty Images; p.9 Kirsty Pargeter/Shutterstock; p.9 (left) JEAN AYISSI/AFP/Getty Images p.9 (right) iStockphoto; p.10 (top) The Print Collector/Alamy; p.10 (bottom) Photos.com; p.11 Mona Lisa Production/Photo Researchers, Inc.; p.12 (top) Bertrand Collet/iStockphoto; p.12 (left) M.I. WALKER/Photo Researchers, Inc.; p.12 (center) Mehau Kulyk/Photo Researchers, Inc.; p.12 (right) Russell Kightley/Photo Researchers, Inc.; p.13 (left) Carlyn Iverson/Photo Researchers, Inc.; p.13 (top) DR. PAUL ANDREWS, UNIVERSITY OF DUNDEE/Photo Researchers, Inc.; p. 13 (bottom) INTERFOTO Pressebildagentur/Alamy; p.14 (top) Sebastian Kaulitzki/Shutterstock; p.14 Carlyn Iverson/Photo Researchers, Inc.; p.15 (top) Keystone/Getty Images; p.15 (bottom) Tim Bradley; p.16 (top) Storman/Shutterstock; p.16 Library of Congress; p.17 (top) Shutterstock; p.17 (bottom) Matt Purciel/Shutterstock; p.18 (top) Public Domain; p.18 (left) Photos.com; p.18 (center) James Steidl/Shutterstock; p.18 (right) Peter Arnold, Inc./Alamy; p.19 Tim Bradley; p.20 PhotoSky 4t com/Shutterstock; p.21 Wendy Shiao/Shutterstock; p.22 (top) iStockphoto; p.22 (left) Bernard Becker Medical Library; p.23 Photos.com; p.24 Lester V. Bergman/CORBIS; p.25 Steve Northup/Time Life Pictures/Getty Images; p.26 (top) Courtesy of Elaine Fuchs; p.26 (bottom) Dr P. Marazzi/Photo Researchers, Inc.; pp.26–27 Lisa F. Young/Shutterstock; pp.26–27 (back) Nici Kuehl/Shutterstock; p27 (left) CNRI/Photo Researchers, Inc.; p.28 (top) Peter Clark/Shutterstock; pp.28–29 Nicolle Rager Fuller; p.32 Getty Images